The
Faith in
Action
Series

Freedom Now!

The Story of Cecilia Flores-Oebanda
and Other Modern-Day Slavery
Abolitionists

Chris Hudson

Illustrated by Paul Bryn Davies

RMEP

RELIGIOUS AND MORAL EDUCATION PRESS

FREEDOM NOW!

The Story of Cecilia Flores-Oebanda and Other Modern-Day Slavery Abolitionists

T he room was full of excited chatter. Strangers came up to her, shook her hand, gave her kisses and congratulated her. Cameras flashed and her name was called from all sides.

Cecilia Flores-Oebanda receiving her award

'Cecilia – this way, please.'
'A big smile? Thank you.'
Cecilia couldn't help but smile; she couldn't keep the grin off her face – she was just so pleased to be here! London was the other side of the world from her home in the Philippines; the weather was cold, but the welcome was so warm! She had made new friends and talked all about the girls she worked with. She *had to* try to remember everything that happened, so that she could tell them when she got back!

Then, the room hushed; the introductions were given and speeches began. When her name was read out, people turned to look.

'Cecilia Flores-Oebanda: winner of the 2005 Anti-Slavery Award.'

She stood up, took a deep breath, and stepped forward into the spotlight to receive the award.

What Do You Think?

Important: In answering 'What Do You Think?' questions in this book, it is important that you not only state your opinion but also give as many reasons as possible for your opinion.

1. What does it mean to be a slave? What is slavery? Give examples of different ways these words are used. You could use a dictionary to help you.

2. Does giving awards benefit a cause? How might Cecilia's award have benefited people other than her?

3. Identify some serious social issues that are found: (a) in your local community, (b) nationally and (c) globally. Which do you think are the most serious? Which of these are personal concerns? Which affect whole communities, or even whole nations?

You can read more about the Anti-Slavery Award on the *Anti-Slavery International* website – www.antislavery.org

A Long-Running Campaign

Over 200 years earlier, in the same city of London, a group of Christians had met together in the district of Clapham. Later known as the *Clapham Sect,* they talked, thought and prayed together about serious social issues. As they were all connected with the *Society for Effecting the Abolition of the Slave Trade* (a campaigning group set up by a number of Quakers and Anglicans), one of their main concerns was the Transatlantic Slave Trade. They all believed that slavery was wrong, and were ashamed that so many white people (many of whom would have called themselves Christians), were involved in the trading of Africans as slaves for the plantations in America and the West Indies. So, they began a campaign to bring an end to the slave trade.

Quakers: a Christian society, founded in the 1600s, whose members meet in quiet to seek God's presence. They are especially active in peace work, human rights and social reform.

Anglicans: members of the Church of England.

It was a difficult struggle, but by 1807, the British Government had been persuaded to ban the trade. This was completed in 1833, with a Parliamentary Act to abolish slavery in all the parts of the world under its control.

How did this happen? Spearheaded by William Wilberforce MP and Thomas Clarkson (an early group member), the successful campaign managed to change the hearts and minds of a whole nation. Clarkson was especially talented at networking with people at every level of society, persuading thousands to voice their concerns and to *do something* to stop the trade. He organised petitions to the government, gathered written evidence, addressed public meetings nationwide, and persuaded famous people to lend their names to the cause. He worked with former slaves like Olaudah Equiano, who had vivid tales to tell of their inhumane experiences, and persuaded William Wilberforce to lead the campaign in Parliament. Finally, the *Act to Abolish the Slave Trade* was passed on 25 March 1807.

When Cecilia Flores-Oebanda stepped forward to receive her award, she was being recognised for her work in campaigning against the conditions of young girls trapped in domestic work in the Philippines – a modern form of slavery. This was very similar to Thomas Clarkson's campaign two centuries earlier. There had been great rejoicing when the British Parliament passed the *Abolition of the Slave Trade Act* in 1807 and many thought that slavery would disappear – but, sadly, it was not the end of the story. Today, it is estimated that there are more people enslaved in different parts of the world now than were enslaved then by the Transatlantic Slave Trade!

Clarkson's *Anti-Slavery Society*, as the *Society for Effecting the Abolition of the Slave Trade* came to be called, continued campaigning about slavery and human rights during the 19th and 20th centuries – and was renamed *Anti-Slavery International* in 1995. Today, its work continues – and it was this organisation that brought Cecilia Flores-Oebanda to London to present her with their 2005 award. Her story is just one part of the global picture of campaigning to abolish slavery.

Cecilia's anti-slavery work is in the same mould as the original campaigns of the 18th and 19th century Christians. She picked up the baton that Clarkson, Equiano and Wilberforce had handed on to others coming after them – and Cecilia is joined by other modern campaigners like her in different parts of the world: people like Cleophas Mally in Togo and Henri Burin des Roziers in Brazil. Just like the first abolitionists, they too believe that slavery is wrong in God's eyes and so they fight to bring it to an end. Modern slavery shows itself in different forms, but the issues remain the same as they were in the 1800s.

Thomas Clarkson

Modern human rights movements such as Make Poverty History owe a lot of their campaigning ideas to the anti-slavery campaign's methods. The Make Poverty History wristband is based on one of those ideas.

Josiah Wedgwood, the potter, created a badge with a simple anti-slavery logo and caption: 'Am I not a man and a brother?' It became a fashion accessory, appearing on brooches, plates and snuff boxes as a way for people to show their support. Thousands were made, sold and given away!

The original anti-slavery campaign also influenced the famous 'sweet tooth' of the British public. The demand for sugar was making a lot of people very rich, but Clarkson urged people to boycott sugar from the slave plantations of the West Indies. Instead, he urged the buying of sugar produced without slave labour.

Nowadays, the Fair Trade movement still uses this method of campaigning. Fair Trade supports workers and small producers in developing countries by monitoring their working conditions, then marketing their goods in the developed world at reasonable prices, not the reduced prices created by some multinational companies. Fairly-traded goods usually cost a little more, but a much greater proportion of the money paid goes to supporting the original producer. Visit www.fairtrade.org.uk for more details.

FAIRTRADE Guarantees a **better deal** for Third World Producers

What Do You Think?

1. What do you think are the best ways of getting a campaign into the public eye? Have you worn a badge or wristband promoting a cause? If so, what made you decide to wear it? If not, ask someone you know about why they chose to support a campaign or organisation in this way.

2. What beliefs might motivate a Christian to work to end slavery? Would these beliefs be shared by: (a) other Christians, (b) people of other religions (say which), (c) non-religious people?

3. What similarities are there between the way campaigners worked to end slavery in the 19th century and modern campaigns against slavery and injustice? What else might campaigners now and then have in common?

Escape from Slavery: Maria's Story

Maria runs down the street, nervously glancing behind to see if she's being followed. No, he isn't there, but he might be pursuing her in the car now. He could be anywhere, just behind her, there on the other side of the road. Should she use the alleyway? No, stay out in the open, where people can see you. He hates making a scene in public! She keeps running. Where to? She glances down at the address she has scribbled down on a piece of paper, the safe place that the girls at the night school told her about. It's three, four blocks away. She stops for breath, checking again to see if she is being followed. No. There's a mother with young children nearby. They stop too, then walk on. The children looked alarmed. Their mother whispers something to them. Walk on. Look away. Don't stare. Stay away from that strange girl. That's the thing to say. Don't ask questions. Maria had said it herself to her employer's children. Don't make a fuss. Look away.

She has her breath back. Maria starts to walk, fast, keeping away from the road with its cars, but still watching the street doors and shop awnings as she approaches them. A policeman stands at the crossing, directing traffic. Talk to him? No. He's another man. Don't trust him.

She crosses the road, walks on, crosses more roads. She's in a part of the city she isn't familiar with, but finally reaches the building she is looking for. Up the steps, ring the bell. Silence, a long silence – then the door opens. She sees a friendly face, a woman's face, inviting her inside. The door closes behind her. It's a cool reception area, with a table, some chairs and a sofa. The friendly face walks towards the sofa, and invites Maria to come and sit next to her. 'You look worried,' says the woman. 'What's the problem?'

Maria sits and tells her story. She talks about how she came to the city at the age of 12 to work as a child domestic, how she has worked for 11 employers, but only one has ever paid her any wages. Then she talks about her current employer, then about the man who tried to kiss her, and worse things, and how she scratched his face and ran down the stairs and out of the house ... and now she doesn't know what to do.

The story comes out gradually, in stages, some of them mixed up, but the friendly face listens attentively. It's a

familiar story in this city. She asks Maria questions and makes notes on a pad.

'What age were you when you started working?'

'Nine.'

'I thought you said 12.'

'That was when I came to this city to work for a new employer.'

'Your salary, you were only ever paid once by somebody?'

'Yes, 500 pesos [about £5] a month.'

'And the work you did?'

'Waking up at 5am to do the household chores, looking after their children, cooking, cleaning, laundry, ironing and looking after pigs.'

'Pigs?'

'That employer had pigs.'

'And where have you lived in this city?'

'Many places, once in a shed with no light or mattress. Those people gave me a fresh pail of water to wash in, every week.'

'And the place where you've just been? The man who tried to kiss you...'

'And worse!'

'Has it happened before?'

'Yes. One of my other employers tried it too, so I left him. He was old, 70 years old, and I was 12. The man who tried it today, he's the brother of my employer.'

'Do you want to go back there?'

'No! No!'

'So... do you want me to find you a safe place to stay? It's temporary, but it's meant for girls like you. It's safe, and you'll have time to work out what you want to do next. We can also give you advice to help you make some good decisions.'

'Yes, please.'

Maria begins to feel safe – for the first time in years.

* *

Slavery still exists in our world – and Maria's escape is a true modern story. The safe house was run by *Visayan Forum*, a national organisation for migrant workers based in the Philippines. Maria heard about them through people she met at her local night school. They sheltered Maria for 6 months and found her some safe work in a small restaurant. After a time, whilst still working, she volunteered to help other girls and took part in outreach campaigns to contact those being abused by their employers. In time, Maria became a local organiser for SUMAPI, the Philippines association for domestic workers. She was made national president of the group and began to study for a degree in psychology, graduating in March 2005. She now works full-time for SUMAPI, training others and expanding the work further.

What Do You Think?

1. When Maria was a child, would you describe her as a slave? Which features of her story make that an appropriate or inappropriate description?

2. How did having somewhere safe to go make a difference to Maria's life?

3. Why do you think Maria didn't trust the policeman? Why did she trust the 'friendly face' who opened the door to her? Who do you turn to for help? How do you decide whom you can trust?

Seek Your Purpose in Life

Maria's escape from slavery was aided by *Visayan Forum*, the Filipino national organisation created by Cecilia Flores-Oebanda. In some ways, you could say that *Visayan Forum* is a modern equivalent of Thomas Clarkson's *Anti-Slavery Society*. For years, Cecilia has successfully campaigned in the Philippines for new laws forbidding the worst forms of child labour and created 'halfway houses' as places of refuge for those escaping domestic abuse. It was for this work that she won the Anti-Slavery Award in 2005 for 'outstanding and innovative work in the Philippines … particularly in the area of child domestic work'. So, how did she get involved?

Cecilia was born into a poor family in a region called the Visayas, in central Philippines. She too was forced to work as a child labourer just to survive. She had to sell fish and scavenge scrap materials from rubbish dumps to raise money for her family. It was, and still is, a hard life for millions like her around the world. Brought up as a Christian, she had noticed how difficult it was for people to escape poverty, no matter how hard they worked. As a teenager, she started doing something about this for herself, working as a catechist in a small

catechist: someone who teaches the Christian faith (usually in the Roman Catholic Church)

chapel where she taught young children in the community. Later she began organising small groups of local people to help them demand better pay from their employers – and land rights for the poor.

By the age of 17, this campaign had become much more dangerous and led her to join rebels fighting to resist the government ruled by the dictator Ferdinand Marcos. He was removed in 1986 in a surprisingly peaceful revolution, but by then, Cecilia (now married and a mother) was quite well known. She was captured and imprisoned as a dangerous threat to national security.

This was very unpleasant and traumatic – but while in prison, a visiting priest befriended Cecilia and advised her to 'Seek your purpose in life.' These words haunted her as she whiled away the weeks and months in the grim prison, and she slowly began to rethink the path her life had taken. Something needed to change. She needed to find a new and different way to fight her battles.

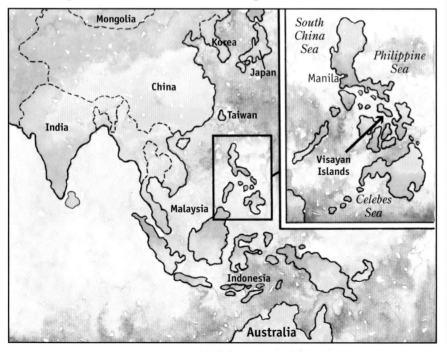

Seek your purpose in life..

When Cecilia was finally released, she went back to working as a fish seller – but, despite the revolution, she saw that many things were still unfair in her country. Was God asking her to serve the people around her in a new way? Poverty, landlessness and armed conflict had forced thousands to migrate to the larger towns and cities in search of a better life – once there, they were easily exploited by anyone who could use (and abuse) a cheap labour force.

So in 1991, Cecilia decided to use all her campaigning skills and passion for justice to make a change: she created a new organisation to bring these migrants together and work for their interests. That was the beginning of *Visayan Forum*.

In 1992, *Visayan Forum* announced it was starting a campaign against the use of child labour. The Philippines is just one country where thousands of children are forced to work, some in factories for very low wages so that goods can be exported and sold very cheaply in countries like the UK.

Visayan Forum has also begun working with hundreds of children, both those living on the streets of the main cities and those – just like Maria – who had been 'trafficked' to become domestic servants in people's homes. Community centres were created to provide education, children's activities, parenting classes and alternative safe ways of generating an income. A domestic workers' association was formed (SUMAPI) and pressure was put on the government to pass a Child Labour Law and an Anti-Trafficking Law.

Cecilia says there is still much more to do in the Philippines. Many people there do not understand why children or poor people need protection and that 'domestic service' can be a dangerous life for many young people.

'I have had a colourful life,' she says. 'You need an anchor aside from your commitment to the issues, a higher anchor of a strong faith and spirituality. You need a greater power to survive in this world, when you see all the abuses that people go through. You cannot be anchored to yourself. I am grateful to God for giving me this journey in life and this purpose of sharing with and serving others.'

Cecilia has made enemies through her work of exposing the cruelty of others and there have been death threats. She says this:

'In hard times, when I feel alone and frustrated, I take a break to reflect and pray. It gives me strength and the ability to conquer my difficulties. I cannot leave my work at *Visayan Forum* as this is what I am meant to do. I will stand firm and continue to fight, and continue to seek my purpose.'

What Do You Think?

1. Have you ever been involved in some action that made a positive difference to someone else's life? Cecilia's Christian faith was a motivation for her work. What motivates you to help other people?

2. Cecilia was told by a priest, 'Seek your purpose in life'. What do you think is your purpose in life? What would you do, or who would you ask, to help you work this out?

3. Is prison a good place to 'take stock' of life? Do people need to be taken out of their normal surroundings to do that? How do you take time to reflect on the big questions in life? Where are your 'thinking spaces'?

4. How does Cecilia's faith help her to carry on with her work? What 'anchors' your life?

The Campaign Against Slavery Continues

In 1833, the *Slave Emancipation Act* was passed by the British Parliament, but the original anti-slavery campaigners didn't stop their work – because slavery didn't stop. Around the world, there was still a great deal more to be done. Throughout the 19th century, other powerful nations had to be persuaded to follow the British lead by changing their own laws. The United States didn't abolish slavery until 1865; in Brazil, the necessary laws weren't passed until 1888.

However, some countries held on to slavery because they were making a lot of money, exploiting the natural riches of their colonies and the people under their control. The Belgian Congo in Africa was brutally ruled and exploited by King Leopold II of Belgium as his personal possession. The outside world knew little about how the Africans who lived there were forced to work as slaves for Leopold's personal profit. It took an international campaign to embarrass rulers like him into stopping the worst examples of their cruelty and exploitation.

One very successful campaigner of this time was George Washington Williams, an African-American who blazed a pioneering trail by going first to university and then to theological college. He became a Baptist minister, a journalist and, for a short while, even entered state politics in the US state of Ohio! He took up the abolitionists' baton, fighting the injustices that continued in America after slavery became illegal.

George ventured across the Atlantic, visiting the Belgian Congo to find out if it would be a suitable place for African-Americans to work. But whilst there, he witnessed the horrors of the continuing use of slaves

colonies: areas of land, or countries, taken over and ruled by the government of another country

The 1833 Act was known officially as the *Act for the Total Abolition of Colonial Slavery*, but is usually known as the *Slave Emancipation Act*. It was passed in 1833 and came into force in August 1834. It gave all slaves in the British Empire their freedom. In reality enslaved Africans in the colonies were forced to work as 'apprentices' for their ex-masters until 1838.

and the dreadful cruelty of their treatment. He was so shocked by what he saw that he coined the phrase 'crimes against humanity'. Using his writing and speaking skills, he immediately challenged King Leopold II to end slavery in his colony – and, with others, brought Leopold's abuses to the attention of the outside world. His words to King Leopold, in 1890, were later published as pamphlets and distributed widely in Europe and the USA:

> *Your Majesty's Government is engaged in the slave-trade, wholesale and retail. It buys and sells and steals slaves. Your Majesty's Government gives £3 per head for able-bodied slaves for military service … The labour force at the stations of your Majesty's Government in the Upper River is composed of slaves of all ages and both sexes.*

George Washington Williams

Just after that, in 1898, the Reverend John Harris and his wife Alice went to the Congo as Baptist missionaries. What they saw shocked them into taking action. Photography was still an exciting new development for their generation, so they began taking photographs, collecting instruments used to punish and restrain slaves, and recording stories of cruelty and ill treatment – including the use of forced labour, murder and the burning of villages.

Afterwards, they reported their findings, speaking at more than 800 public meetings across Europe and the USA. Their powerful photographs and displays of slave-shackles took the realities of life in the Congo right into the homes and meeting rooms of many influential people. The images were undeniable and unavoidable. This was a new type of anti-slavery campaign.

When John and Alice Harris returned to the Congo in 1912, they were able to report that the situation had improved. King Leopold II had handed over responsibility to the Belgian Government and the anti-slavery campaigns had begun to bear fruit!

However, a big question remains – was Christianity *in favour* of slavery before the 18th century campaigners? Up to that point,

Transatlantic slavery had gone relatively unchallenged by white Europeans, many of whom were Christians. Many Christian Churches in Europe were involved in slavery – some church buildings were constructed from the profits of slave cargoes. Slavery *was* thought to be moral and legal. Today, however, it is universally acknowledged to be immoral *and* illegal, although different forms of slavery *do still* exist. That's why Cecilia Flores-Oebanda, and others like her, *still* have to campaign against the trafficking of people and the abuse and neglect of workers by their employers. Where slavery exists, money and power are always involved.

Photo © Anti-Slavery International

Slaves in chains photographed in the Belgian Congo by Alice and John Harris in 1904

In 1948, after the horrors of the Second World War, the Universal Declaration of Human Rights was written and agreed by all the countries in the United Nations. It specifically spoke out against slavery in any form.

Yet across the 21st century world, including Europe, forms of slavery can still be found, despite it being illegal. Usually the people who become slaves are vulnerable, poor or desperate. Often they are victims of criminal gangs who make a lot of money from the trade. 'Trafficking' is what happens when men, women and children are taken from their homes by force or deception, transported some distance (similar to the Transatlantic Slave Trade), then forced to work for little or no money. Many are exploited by being forced into prostitution or domestic work and, in some parts of the world, enslaved children are even forced to fight as soldiers. This is why local campaigning organisations like the *Visayan Forum* in the Philippines are so important – they speak up for those who have no voice. They remind the politicians of their duty to protect the poor and the weak, and remind employers of their duties to protect their workers.

Article 1.
All human beings are born free and equal in dignity and rights. They are endowed with reason and conscience and should act towards one another in a spirit of brotherhood.

Article 3.
Everyone has the right to life, liberty and security of person.

Article 4.
No one shall be held in slavery or servitude; slavery and the slave trade shall be prohibited in all their forms.

Article 5.
No one shall be subjected to torture or to cruel, inhuman or degrading treatment or punishment.

Extracts from the Universal Declaration of Human Rights (December 1948)

What Do You Think?

1. The phrase 'crimes against humanity' is often used today. What might it describe? Do you think it is a good term to use? Give reasons.

2. What kinds of people are most in danger of becoming slaves? What do you think can be done about this?

3. John and Alice Harris used photographic images to shock people into action. Today shocking images are everywhere, in newspapers, on TV and the internet and in films. Can you think of recent examples when such images have moved people to action? Why are there times when people ignore shocking images?

4. In the 18th century, slavery was legal and considered to be moral by most people. Are there things today that are legal but which you consider to be immoral? Give reasons.

Child Labour and Slavery

The cheapest way to get a job done is to pay the worker very little – or even nothing at all. Children have always been employed in a variety of ways around the world for very low wages. This can generate important income for poor families and be a valuable source of training (e.g., apprenticeships), but the work conditions can be dangerous and unhealthy, the child usually misses out on their education – and their immaturity makes them vulnerable to all sorts of cruelties. It's just slavery in a different form.

As Cecilia Flores-Oebanda stood beaming at the photographers while they scooped their press photos, she was reminded of other

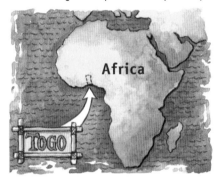

pictures – the faces of children, the hundreds of young people helped by her organisation. And she thought about other campaigners like Lord Shaftesbury in England in the 19th century and Cleophas Mally, in Togo, still campaigning in the 21st century. There were so many faces and so many stories.

In Great Britain, Christians and politicians like Lord Shaftesbury led campaigns in the 19th century to restrict and regulate the use of children in dangerous occupations such as coal-mining and sweeping chimneys by climbing up the inside. These campaigners were often criticised for trying to improve the lives of the 'undeserving poor' – just as the original campaigners against the slave trade were attacked for challenging practices that made Britain rich.

A Logical Problem: One Boy's Story

Marcus couldn't concentrate. His new maths teacher, Mr Dupont, was puzzled. All the other boys were sitting at their desks, quietly concentrating on the problems in their textbooks and scribbling answers down, but Marcus was just sitting there, listless, fiddling with his pencil and staring out of the window at nothing.

It was all a bit of a puzzle. According to school records, the boy was bright and used to getting good test results, but things had gone downhill a year after he entered the junior school. Why? Hadn't he come from a good family? Apparently, there were some upsets at home – something about the parents having to leave the country, but his uncle had stepped in to care for him. In Africa, there's usually someone in the wider family nearby who can help in a crisis.

Mr Dupont shrugged to himself. He couldn't solve family problems for his pupils – he could only teach them to solve the mathematical ones.

There was a knock at the door and a smartly-dressed stranger walked in. He approached Mr Dupont's desk, and held out his hand.

'I'm Marcus's uncle. I need a word with him.'

'Of course!' replied the teacher, shaking his hand.

'Could I see you afterwards? I'm a little concerned about his progress.'

'Yes. Excuse me. I'll see him now.'

The teacher went back to his marking. The stranger walked between the rows of desks and stopped by Marcus, who was staring up at him, sitting bolt upright, unblinking.

'Marcus', said his uncle. 'You know what I've come to see you about.'

Marcus looked away. There was a sudden scraping of furniture and a yelling. Mr Dupont glanced up in horror. The uncle had grabbed Marcus by the ear and was beating him hard all over his head and body with a knotted rope. It must have been concealed in a pocket.

'*This* will teach you to do your jobs before you come to school!' yelled the uncle. *'What have I told you, you ungrateful little worm?'* The classroom erupted in chaos as students scrambled away. Mr Dupont fought his way through just as the uncle had released the boy, who now lay slumped on the floor, his arms covering his head. The man turned towards the teacher, his face now twisted in anger.

'Was there something you wanted to ask me about, Mr Dupont?' he snarled. There was a shocked silence, then a whispered reply.

'No.' Another pause, then a firm 'But I think you should leave – now'.

The stranger did so without another word, his angry footsteps echoing along the corridor. After a moment's shocked silence, Mr Dupont sent one student off to see the Head to explain what had just happened, sent the others back to their desks, then took Marcus out into the corridor to calm down. So this was why he couldn't work at school! The boy was being used as an unpaid domestic servant and he was terrified! What could be done? It was difficult – a tougher puzzle than anything found in any textbook.

Speaking Up for the Children

Cleophas Mally still vividly remembers being treated like a slave when he was a child and it has directed his life ever since. Born in Togo, West Africa, in the 1950s, Cleophas's childhood was happy at first. He describes it like this:

Cleophas Mally

Photo courtesy *Anti-Slavery International*

'I was living in a good environment with all the benefits of a son of a government minister. At the age of 8, my life changed. My father was forced into exile with my mother, after the army took over the country. I was then placed under the care of my uncle, whom I served as a domestic worker. For me, it was like leaving Heaven for Hell. As a domestic child, I experienced all sorts of maltreatment – for example, I had to be the first to wake up, the last to go to bed, fetching water for the whole family, doing all types of household work and so on. This continued until 1968 when my parents came back from exile.

'Interestingly, despite the terrible living conditions, I continued to go to school. I always prayed for God to protect me against all these sufferings and for other children, whom I realised suffered much more than me. All these things touched me a lot. But my faith has given me confidence and I know and believe that God loves and protects children and slaves.'

Tens of thousands of children are still trafficked into slavery-like conditions in West Africa each year. The largest single employing sector is domestic work, the workers mostly being girls aged as young as 5 years old.

Since 1989, Cleophas Mally has used his own childhood experiences to fuel a campaign to end child labour and trafficking, working with *WAO-Afrique*, a campaigning organisation that promotes and protects children's rights both in Togo and throughout Africa. A regional counter-trafficking network has been set up, aiding the release of hundreds of children from intolerable working conditions and returning them to their families. The working conditions of over 1000 children have been improved, and hundreds of school-age children have been rescued from domestic work and provided with education.

Like the anti-slavery campaigners of the 18th century, *WAO-Afrique* has used a multi-layered approach to solving the problem of child slavery, involving:

· continued detailed research into what is actually happening

· raising public awareness that pressurises governments to act on the problem

· providing a network to help victims escape their suffering

Cleophas has received death threats from those who profit from child labour and trafficking – but also international recognition for his work. In 1995, the magazine *Jeune Afrique Economique* declared him as their 'Man of the Year' for his efforts to benefit the children of Togo. *Plan International* gave him an award for services to the child victims of domestic work and he was also a recipient at the *Body Shop Human Rights Awards* in 2000. He still campaigns with *WAO-Afrique* today.

Freedom Now!

15

Child Labour: How Big is the Problem?

Nowadays, the use of child labour is a big issue for developing countries. Growing businesses need to manufacture products for export at the cheap prices demanded by people living in the rest of the world. That leads factories to employ children for very low wages.

- The *International Labour Organization* estimates there are 246 million working children aged between 5 and 17
- 179 million are estimated to work in the worst forms of child labour – one in every eight of the world's 5 to 17 year olds
- 111 million children under 15 are in hazardous work and should be 'immediately withdrawn from this work'
- 8.4 million children are in slavery, trafficking, debt bondage and other forms of forced labour, forced recruitment for armed conflict, prostitution, pornography and other illicit activities
- Girls are particularly in demand for domestic work

Source: Anti-Slavery International

It's not just factories. Children can be used and abused in other global businesses such as tourism, sport and leisure. When Ahmed was 5 years old he was trafficked from Bangladesh to the United Arab Emirates to be a camel jockey. He was forced to train and race camels in Dubai for three years.

'I was scared … If I made a mistake I was beaten with a stick. When I said I wanted to go home I was told I never would. I didn't enjoy camel racing, I was really afraid. I fell off many times. When I won prizes, such as money and a car, the camel owner took everything. I never got anything, no money, nothing; my family also got nothing.'

Ahmed was returned home only after a Bangladeshi official identified him during a visit to Dubai in November 2002.

'Child labour has serious consequences that stay with the individual and with society for far longer than the years of childhood. Young workers not only face dangerous working conditions. They face long term physical, intellectual and emotional stress. They face an adulthood of unemployment and illiteracy.'

Kofi Annan
United Nations Secretary General

Photo courtesy Anti-Slavery International/CDP

Child jockey camel racing in Dubai

Child Soldiers

In war zones around the world today, children are caught up in the fighting, often forced to join armies in near slave conditions. There are about 300 000 child soldiers (some younger than 10 years old) involved in over 30 areas of conflict worldwide. Children are captured and frequently drugged so that they are easily manipulated and will obey orders. The drugs can make them much more aggressive and willing to fight. The experiences of a boy soldier in Liberia are typical:

Often the fighters smoke opium; I took tablets. That gave me courage to fight. I was always brave. We broke into food shops to steal food. Sometimes the people were killed because they did not give us food.

Child soldiers may fight on the front line or work in support roles; girls are often obliged to be 'soldiers' wives'. The children involved in these conflicts are severely affected by their experiences afterwards.

Christian Aid and *World Vision* are just two Christian charities amongst many mediating between rebels and governments fighting in unstable parts of the world. They also rehabilitate child soldiers in areas of conflict by providing safe places of refuge, counselling and education, and, where possible, reuniting the children with their families.

christian **aid**   We believe in life before death

World Vision

What Do You Think?

1. How does knowing that so many children are exploited as child workers in today's world make you feel? Do you think forcing children to work can ever be justified? Why?/Why not?

2. What effects might being a child soldier have on that person later in life?

A Legacy of the Transatlantic Slave Trade

One legacy of the Transatlantic Slave Trade in South America is that many people of African descent living there continue to be very poor – so they are easily exploited. This form of racism is still common, particularly in Brazil, where many enslaved Africans were taken to work on plantations. Despite slavery being outlawed by the end of the 19th century, some powerful landowners still work their labourers in conditions of near-slavery – because they can get away with it.

In Brazil it sometimes works like this:

Imagine you come from a poor family. You answer an advertisement for what seems like a good farming job some distance away – and sign on.

You are taken by truck to a remote area. On arrival, you are told you owe money for your transport, accommodation, food and equipment, and that you must work to pay back the debt.

The debt, the remoteness of the farms and the frequent threats and violence from your employers then trap you into a form of slavery, working long hours for little or no pay. Ruled over by gang bosses with guns, there seems no escape.

In the 1970s, the Catholic Church began asking itself what Christians should do when human rights were being ignored by those in power. Would Jesus be in favour of fighting for social justice? 'Yes!' they decided, and began challenging both the landowners and the government they supported. Then in 1975, the Bishops' Council founded the *Pastoral Land Commission*. Members such as Henri Burin des Roziers have supported rural people in land disputes with big landowners, and even started taking employers to court over disputes with their workers.

There has been progress. Slavery's legal definition was tightened up by the Brazilian Government to make prosecutions easier – and a so-called 'black list' was created of companies using slave labour, which blocked them from claiming government grants. More slave labourers have been freed by the Special Mobile Inspection Group, which was set up in 1995 to make raids on estates where slavery was being used.

But people like Henri Burin des Roziers live in fear of their lives. Henri, a French lawyer and Catholic priest, has fought tirelessly to free people from the slave labour conditions. Like the anti-slavery campaigners in England in the 18th century, he tackles politicians, wealthy landowners and gang bosses. Working with escaped slaves, Henri helps bring plantation owners and gang bosses to court. But it is a dangerous business – and Henri is a marked man! In January 2003, three labour inspectors and their driver were murdered during a routine inspection. Local judges, prosecutors and human rights activists (like Henri) face numerous threats – and those who are charged with 'using slave labour' generally receive low sentences or small fines, which usually go unpaid.

One state prosecutor says: 'There is still so, so, so much slavery. It is part of the culture.' And the wealthy landowners and business people don't want that to change. They are powerful people, using money and guns to keep the status quo. There is still a lot to do to abolish this type of slavery.

What Do You Think?

1. What do you think the prosecutor meant by saying: 'There is still so, so, so much slavery. It is part of the culture'? What could be done to change this?

2. People and resources can both be exploited. What do you think that means? Is it possible to accept Jesus' teaching to 'love your neighbour as yourself' and to exploit others? Why?/Why not?

Fighting Slavery Goes On...

As a young girl, Cecilia Flores-Oebanda had to work hard to support her family. Cleophas Mally was also exploited as a child domestic worker. Drawing on their own experiences, they have both followed in the footsteps of the former slave Olaudah Equiano. Two hundred years before them, Equiano used his own experiences and story to campaign for the 1807 *Act to Abolish the Slave Trade*. Today, just like the earlier abolitionists Thomas Clarkson and William Wilberforce, Henri Burin des Roziers uses his professional background to campaign for freedom of slaves in South America.

These three 21st century campaigners, inspired by their belief that God intended all people to be equal and free, have been recognised with international awards for their work and bravery. Many other activists remain unrecognised and unknown, but they all continue to campaign because the fight to abolish slavery is not yet won!

What Do You Think?

1. If someone campaigning against slavery has experienced slavery themselves, what influence might this have on their action to end slavery – e.g. what advantages or disadvantages might it give them? Think about the different campaigners, past and present, in this book.

2. Modern campaigners (a) use detailed research into what is happening, (b) raise public awareness and so put pressure on governments, (c) provide a means of escape for those suffering. What would be the effect of missing out one of these elements of the campaign? Which do you think is most important? Give reasons.

Time-line

1790s	William Wilberforce, Thomas Clarkson and others campaign to abolish the slave trade.
1807	British Parliament passes the *Act to Abolish the Slave Trade*.
1833	The *Slave Emancipation Act* passed in Britain.
1865	United States abolishes slavery.
1888	Brazil abolishes slavery.
1890	George Washington Williams visits the Belgian Congo.
1898	John and Alice Harris go to the Belgian Congo as missionaries. They take photographs to use in the campaign against slavery.
1912	John and Alice Harris return to the Congo and report that improvements have taken place.
1926	League of Nations Slavery Convention.
1948	Universal Declaration of Human Rights.
1950s	Cleophas Mally a child in Togo, West Africa.
1956	The UN Supplementary Convention on the Abolition of Slavery, the Slave Trade and Institutions and Practices Similar to Slavery.
1968	Cleophas' parents return from exile.
1975	The Catholic Bishops' Council found the *Pastoral Land Commission* in Brazil.
1977	Henri Burin des Roziers begins working as a lawyer for the Pastoral Land Commission in Brazil.
1986	Removal of dictator Ferdinand Marcos of the Philippines.
1989	Cleophas Mally begins a campaign to end child labour and trafficking in Togo.
1991	Cecilia Flores-Oebanda creates *Visayan Forum* in the Philippines to bring migrants together and to work for their interests.
1992	*Visayan Forum* begins campaigning against the use of child labour in the Philippines.
1995	Cleophas Mally is declared 'Man of the Year' by *Jeune Afrique Economique* for his efforts to benefit the children of Togo. He receives the *Plan International* award for his services to the child victims of domestic work.
1999	Henri Burin des Roziers included on a list of people 'destined for death'.
2000	Cleophas Mally receives *Body Shop Human Rights Award*.
2000	United Nations Protocol to Prevent, Suppress and Punish Trafficking in Persons, Especially Women and Children.
2003	Philippine Congress passes Anti-Trafficking Act.
2005	Henri Burin des Roziers wins the International Human Rights Prize.
2005	Cecilia Flores-Oebanda wins the *Anti-Slavery Award*.

Things to Do

1

EITHER

Create a storyboard for a TV documentary about Cecilia's life, paying special attention to the key moments in the story. What messages do you want to communicate in your film? What would be its title and how would you advertise it?

OR

Cecilia and others, past and present, have used their experiences in the campaign against slavery. In groups, choose one person who has used their life story to help them campaign for change. Research their life story, then prepare a 5 minute presentation for the class, showing clearly what they believed and how using their story strengthened their campaign.

2

What is slavery? Think about the different examples of slavery, past and present, in this book.

(a) List features that are common to all forms of slavery.

(b) List features that apply to some examples of slavery but not others.

(c) Write dictionary definitions of the words 'slave' and 'slavery' that cover these different forms of slavery. You could present your answers as an illustrated diagram or table.

3

(a) Rewrite the extracts from the Universal Declaration of Human Rights on page 12 in your own words. Do you agree with them? What other rights do you think human beings should have? Write a list and then check against the full version (www.un.org/overview/rights.html) to see if they are included.

(b) What can happen to people when they are denied their rights? Give examples.

4

In pairs, imagine you are radio journalists planning an interview with a child slave.

(a) Decide what sort of programme the interview is for, what type of audience it will have and the message you want to get across.

(b) List questions to ask in order to give listeners an idea of what the child's life is like. Which aspects will you emphasise?

(c) Use your imagination to write the child's responses and/or record the interview, each taking one of the parts.

5 Find out more about organisations which campaign against slavery today. *Anti-Slavery International* is one which traces its foundation back to the abolitionists of the 16th and 17th centuries (www.antislavery.org).

6 (a) Find out more about Henri Burin des Roziers' work and the Brazilian *Pastoral Land Commission* on the Internet. Search for Henri Burin des Roziers and Brazilian Pastoral Land Commission in a search engine.

(b) Imagine a wealthy landowner who is using slave labour is on trial in a court in Brazil. Plan the prosecutor's questions and the defendant's answers. What witnesses could the prosecution use? What evidence could they give? How might the landowner defend him/herself? What could be done to help make sure that the trial is fair?

7 Discuss or reflect on what motivates people to risk or devote their lives to campaign against things like slavery.

· Why do they do it and what helps them continue their fight when things get tough?

· What difference may it make if the campaigner has a religious faith?

· Write an acrostic poem using the word MOTIVATION to express your ideas.

8 (a) Why do some people ignore unjust situations, turn a 'blind eye' and say, 'It's nothing to do with me'? Think of as many different reasons as you can.

(b) Give examples concerning slavery to support the statement: 'The love of money is the root of all evil'.

(c) List different methods used by anti-slavery campaigners, past and present, to make an impact, raise awareness and change people's attitudes and behaviour. Which were most effective and why? What other strategies could campaigners have tried? Are there any methods which you think should not be used to campaign against injustice? Give reasons.

9 Find out about the effect of the Fair Trade movement on producers, consumers and companies. What arguments do people use to justify not using fairly traded goods? How could you combat those views? Design a poster to convince consumers to use fairly traded goods. Make sure it conveys at least one clear reason why this is a positive thing to do.

Some of the following websites may be helpful:
www.fairtrade.org.uk
www.traidcraft.org.uk
www.christian-aid.org.uk
www.oxfam.org.uk
www.cafod.org.uk
www.wvi.org

10 Imagine you are mounting a campaign to end child labour. What kinds of things will you need to do? What messages will you need to communicate? Draft an overall plan for your campaign. Choose one section of the plan and give some detail about what you would do.

Useful websites to find out more include:
www.antislavery.org
www.setallfree.net
www.fairtrade.org.uk
www.makepovertyhistory.org
www.jubileedebtcampaign.org.uk

11 In groups, research and plan a class presentation about asylum seekers. Find out about:

· Asylum seekers' backgrounds and different reasons why they fled their countries.

· What sort of life do they have now? How are they treated by the authorities and by people in areas where they live?

· What are Churches doing to help asylum seekers?

Identify links with experiences and situations described in this book.

Religious and Moral Education Press
A division of SCM-Canterbury Press Ltd
A wholly owned subsidiary of
Hymns Ancient & Modern Ltd
St Mary's Works, St Mary's Plain
Norwich, Norfolk NR3 3BH

First published 2007

ISBN 978 1 85175 343 7

Designed and typeset by
TOPICS – The Creative Partnership, Exeter

Printed in Great Britain by Brightsea Press, Exeter for SCM-Canterbury Press Ltd, Norwich

Notes for Teachers

The first *Faith in Action* books were published in the late 1970s and the series has remained popular with both teachers and pupils. However, much in education has changed over the last twenty years, such as the development of both new examination syllabuses in Religious Studies and local agreed syllabuses for Religious Education which place more emphasis on pupils' own understanding, interpretation and evaluation of religious belief and practice, rather than a simple knowledge of events. This has encouraged us to amend the style of the *Faith in Action* Series to make it more suitable for today's classroom.

The aim is, as before, to tell the stories of people who have lived and acted according to their faith, but we have included alongside the main story questions which will encourage pupils to think about the reasons for the behaviour of our main characters and to empathise with the situations in which they found themselves. We hope that pupils will also be able to relate some of the issues in the stories to other issues in modern society, either in their own area or on a global scale.

The 'What Do You Think?' questions may be used for group or class discussion or for short written exercises. The 'Things to Do' at the end of the story include ideas for longer activities for RE or Citizenship and offer opportunities for assessment.

In line with current syllabus requirements, as Britain is a multifaith society, Faith in Action characters are selected from a variety of faith backgrounds and many of the questions may be answered from the perspective of more than one faith.

Acknowledgements

This is one of three *Faith in Action* books and a Teacher's Resource on CD-ROM published in association with **set all free** ACT TO END SLAVERY, a project of Churches Together in England to commemorate the bicentenary in 2007 of the *Act to Abolish the Slave Trade*. Further information can be found at www.setallfree.net

These publications have been developed by the **set all free** education group, consisting of Uzoamaka Agyare-Kumi, Linda Ali, Alison Farnell, Sarah Lane, Tessa Oram, Richard Reddie, Sally Smith and Kate Yates, who have all made significant contributions to the content.

Staff at The Stapleford Centre have helped to produce this series – www.stapleford-centre.org

We are grateful to Cecilia Flores-Oebanda, Sarah Williams and staff at *Anti-Slavery International* for help with ideas, information and research for the content of this book, and for providing images to be used in this publication. To join the campaign to make slavery a thing of the past once and for all, visit www.antislavery.org